EDGARTOWN
Free Public Library

T HE REFLECTIONS and histories of men and
women throughout the world are contained
in books. . . . America's greatness is not only re-
corded in books, but it is also dependent upon
each and every citizen being able to utilize public
libraries.

— Terence Cooke

Presented by

58 North Water St. ❧ P.O. Box 5429
Edgartown, Mass. 02539

Edgartown
PUBLIC
LIBRARY

QUICK & EASY CURRIES

Comments

Please share your thoughts about this book with the next borrower. Thank you!

_____

_____

_____

_____

_____

_____

_____

_____

How do you rate this book?

EXCELLENT	GOOD	FAIR	POOR

QUICK & EASY
CURRIES

Consultant Editor:
Valerie Ferguson

LORENZ BOOKS

Contents

Introduction

The popularity of curries continues to grow and now we enjoy dishes not only from India and Pakistan, but also from South-east Asia – Thailand, Malaysia and Indonesia. Indian curries, such as Chicken Madras and Aloo Saag, use carefully blended dried and freshly ground spices and tend to be thick. Balti curries, such as Balti Keema with Curry Leaves & Green Chillies, are hot and speedily stir-fried, traditionally in a two-handled pan known as a *karahi*. South-east Asian curries rely more on "wet" spices, which may be pounded into a paste – lemon grass, kaffir lime leaves, fresh coriander (cilantro) galangal, and fresh chillies. Such dishes include Malaysian Fish Curry and Thai Tofu Curry.

Today, we do not have to travel far to eat curries from any of these regions, as a wide variety of spices, Oriental vegetables and other special ingredients are available in Western supermarkets, enabling us to recreate a whole range of authentic-tasting dishes at home. Best of all, many of them take little time to prepare but are still bursting with flavour. This book draws together a selection of the most delicious, quick-to-make curry recipes, offering a kaleidoscope of textures and tastes, from mild and fragrant to fiery hot.

Ingredients

Chicken & Meat

Lamb, chicken and beef are widely used in Indian and balti curries, while beef tends to be the preferred meat in South-east Asia.

Dairy Produce & Oils

Plain yogurt is often added to milder Indian and balti curries, creating a creamy sauce; it is also combined with cucumber and mint to make a wonderfully cooling raita, served as an accompaniment to fiery-hot dishes. Paneer, a pressed curd cheese, is cubed and used in combination with seafood, chicken and vegetables in balti curries, providing extra protein. Ghee (clarified butter) was once the main cooking fat used in Indian and Pakistani cooking, but it is often replaced nowadays with groundnut or corn oil.

Fish

Monkfish, red snapper and cod are widely used. Shellfish, such as prawns (shrimp), mussels and clams, feature in many dishes, especially in coastal regions where they are plentiful.

Flavourings

In South-east Asia fish sauce, soy sauce and terasi (fermented shrimp paste, sold in blocks) are popular flavourings. Coconut products, including milk and cream, provide a distinctive creaminess and taste.

Above: Lentils, nuts and flavourings found in many Asian dishes.

Grains, Lentils, Pulses & Tofu

These all play an important role in Eastern cooking. Rice, in its various forms, is served universally as an accompaniment to curries, though it may be replaced by noodles – egg, rice, bean thread or cellophane – in South-east Asia. Breads, such as naan, paratha and chapatti, are frequently served with Indian curries.

Lentils are often used in Indian and Pakistani cuisine. These include chana and toor dhal (split yellow lentils), masoor dhal (split red) and urid dhal (blackish). Commonly eaten pulses include black-eyed beans, kidney beans and chickpeas.

Tofu (soya beancurd) is a popular protein food in South-east Asia: the firm kind is cut into cubes before being added to dishes.

Above: Fresh seafood, vegetables and rice, often used in Asian cuisine.

Herbs

Garlic and fresh coriander (cilantro) are widely used. Mint is an important ingredient in raita, and is also used as a flavouring for poultry dishes.

Fenugreek leaves, which add a slightly bitter flavour, are sometimes called for in balti recipes (the seeds are also used in small quantities, whole or ground). South-east Asian cooking is characterized by its use of aromatic lemon grass and kaffir lime leaves.

Nuts

Cashews and peanuts feature in Indian cooking. Almonds may be used whole, ground as a thickener or flaked and toasted as a garnish. Peanuts are a popular addition to Thai dishes.

Spices

The cuisines of India and Pakistan use a wide range of spices. Aromatic cardamom pods are added whole to rice and meat dishes; they should be removed before serving.

Fresh and dried chillies and chilli powder provide heat. Cinnamon brings a warm spiciness to savoury and sweet dishes. The whole or ground seeds of coriander, one of the most popular spices, add a slightly sweet flavour, while cumin seeds, again whole or ground, have a strong, musky taste.

Curry leaves are the Indian version of bay leaves. Sharp and refreshing root ginger and lemony galangal, which should be peeled before use, are usually sliced or grated. Black mustard seeds bring a nutty flavour to vegetables and pulses. Freshly grated nutmeg has a sweet, nutty taste, and tamarind adds a strong sourness to dishes. Turmeric is used primarily for

Above: Colourful fresh vegetables play a major part in many Asian dishes.

its bright yellow colouring and it has a slightly bitter, spicy taste.

Several of these spices are combined to produce garam masala, the main dry spice mixture in Indian cooking and red or green curry paste for Thai dishes.

Vegetables

Fresh vegetables are indispensable in Indian, Pakistani and South-east Asian cooking. Frequently used vegetables include onions, potatoes, spinach and red and green peppers. Tomatoes, an essential of Indian and balti food, are widely used to make all sorts of sauces, chutneys and relishes. Another Indian favourite is okra (ladies' fingers) which has a very distinctive flavour and a sticky, pulpy texture when cooked. Peas, beans, cauliflower and mushrooms are also popular.

Garam Masala

This spicy powder is added at the end of cooking.

Makes about 50 g/2 oz

INGREDIENTS
10 dried red chillies
3 x 2.5 cm/1 in cinnamon sticks
2 curry leaves
30 ml/2 tbsp coriander seeds
30 ml/2 tbsp cumin seeds
5 ml/1 tsp black peppercorns
5 ml/1 tsp cloves
5 ml/1 tsp fenugreek seeds
5 ml/1 tsp black mustard seeds
1.5 ml/¼ tsp chilli powder

1 Dry-roast the chillies, cinnamon and curry leaves in a heavy-based frying pan for 2 minutes. Add the remaining whole spices and dry-roast for a further 8–10 minutes, shaking the pan frequently.

2 Cool slightly, then grind to a fine powder using a coffee grinder or pestle and mortar. Mix in the chilli powder. Store in an airtight jar.

Curry Paste

A "wet" blend of cooked spices, convenient for adding to recipes.

Makes about
600 ml/1 pint/2½ cups

INGREDIENTS
50 g/2 oz/½ cup coriander seeds
60 ml/4 tbsp cumin seeds
30 ml/2 tbsp fennel seeds
30 ml/2 tbsp fenugreek seeds
4 dried red chillies
5 curry leaves
15 ml/1 tbsp chilli powder
15 ml/1 tbsp turmeric
150 ml/¼ pint/⅔ cup white wine vinegar
250 ml/8 fl oz/1 cup oil

1 Grind all the whole spices to a fine powder. Spoon into a bowl and add the remaining ground spices. Mix to a thin paste with the vinegar and add 75 ml/5 tbsp water.

2 Stir-fry the paste in the oil for 10 minutes or until the water has been absorbed. When the oil rises to the surface, the paste is cooked. Cool slightly before spooning into sterilized jars.

Indonesian Fish Curry

This simple dish is packed with many characteristic flavours associated with the cuisine of the region.

Serves 4–6

INGREDIENTS
675 g/1½ lb cod or haddock fillet
1 cm/½ in cube terasi
2 red or white onions
2 garlic cloves
2.5 cm/1 in fresh root ginger, peeled
   and sliced
1 cm/½ in fresh galangal, peeled and sliced,
   or 5 ml/1 tsp galangal powder
1–2 red chillies, seeded,
   or 5–10 ml/1–2 tsp chilli powder
90 ml/6 tbsp sunflower oil
15 ml/1 tbsp dark soy sauce
5 ml/1 tsp tamarind pulp, soaked in
   30 ml/2 tbsp warm water
250 ml/8 fl oz/1 cup water
celery leaves or chopped chilli, to garnish
boiled rice, to serve

1 Skin the fish, remove any bones and cut the flesh into bite-size pieces. Pat dry with kitchen paper and set aside.

2 Grind the terasi, onions, garlic, ginger, fresh galgangal and chillies, if using, to a paste in a food processor or with a pestle and mortar. Stir in the chilli and galangal powders, if using.

VARIATION: 450 g/1 lb cooked tiger prawns (large shrimp) can replace the fish, added at the end.

3 Heat 30 ml/2 tbsp of the oil in a heavy-based frying pan and fry the spice mixture, stirring, until it gives off a rich aroma. Add the soy sauce. Strain the tamarind and add the juice and water. Cook for 2–3 minutes.

4 In a separate pan, fry the fish in the remaining oil for 2–3 minutes. Turn once only so that the pieces stay whole. Lift out with a slotted spoon and put into the sauce.

5 Cook the fish in the sauce for a further 3 minutes. Serve with boiled rice and garnish with celery leaves or a little chopped fresh chilli.

Spicy Fish Fillets

A delicious spicy coconut sauce coats the fish in this quick curry.

Serves 4

INGREDIENTS

30 ml/2 tbsp corn oil
5 ml/1 tsp onion seeds
4 dried red chillies
3 garlic cloves, sliced
1 medium onion, sliced
2 medium tomatoes, sliced
30 ml/2 tbsp desiccated coconut
5 ml/1 tsp salt
5 ml/1 tsp ground coriander
4 flat fish fillets, each about 75 g/3 oz
150 ml/¼ pint/⅔ cup water
30 ml/1 tbsp lime juice
30 ml/1 tbsp chopped fresh coriander
  (cilantro)
boiled rice, to serve

1 Heat the oil in a wok or heavy-based frying pan. Lower the heat slightly and add the onion seeds, chillies, garlic and onion. Cook for 3–4 minutes, stirring once or twice. Add the tomatoes, coconut, salt and ground coriander and stir thoroughly.

2 Cut each fish fillet into three pieces and drop them into the mixture. Turn them over gently until well coated.

3 Cook for 5–7 minutes, lowering the heat if necessary. Add the water, lime juice and fresh coriander and cook for a further 3–5 minutes until the water has almost evaporated. Serve immediately with rice.

Malaysian Fish Curry

Lemon grass, galangal, chillies and coconut give flavour to this tasty dish.

Serves 4–6

INGREDIENTS
675 g/1½ lb monkfish or red snapper fillet
45 ml/3 tbsp desiccated coconut
30 ml/2 tbsp vegetable oil
2.5 cm/1 in galangal, peeled and thinly sliced
2 small red chillies, seeded and finely chopped
2 garlic cloves, crushed
5 cm/2 in lemon grass, shredded
1 cm/½ in cube shrimp paste
400 g/14 oz can coconut milk
600 ml/1 pint/2½ cups chicken stock
2.5 ml/½ tsp ground turmeric
15 ml/1 tbsp sugar
juice of 1 lime
salt
lime slices and coriander, to garnish
boiled rice, to serve

1 Skin and bone the fish. Cut into large chunks and season with salt. Dry fry the coconut in a wok or heavy-based frying pan until evenly brown. Add the oil, galangal, chillies, garlic and lemon grass and fry briefly. Stir in the shrimp paste.

2 Strain the coconut milk and add the thin part to the wok. Add the stock, turmeric, sugar, some salt and the lime juice. Simmer for 10 minutes.

3 Add the fish and allow to simmer for 6–8 minutes. Stir in the thick coconut milk and simmer. Garnish the curry with lime and coriander and serve with rice.

13

Paneer Balti with Prawns

The intriguing combination of textures and flavours in this curry is a delight to the palate. Delicious served with plain rice.

Serves 4

INGREDIENTS
12 cooked king prawns (jumbo shrimp)
175 g/6 oz paneer cheese
30 ml/2 tbsp tomato purée (paste)
60 ml/4 tbsp Greek (US strained plain)
    yogurt
25 ml/1½ tbsp garam masala
5 ml/1 tsp chilli powder
5 ml/1 tsp crushed garlic
5 ml/1 tsp salt
10 ml/2 tsp mango powder
5 ml/1 tsp ground coriander
115 g/4 oz/½ cup butter or ghee
15 ml/1 tbsp corn oil
3 green chillies, chopped
45 ml/3 tbsp chopped
    fresh coriander (cilantro)
150 ml/¼ pint/⅔ cup single (light) cream

1 Peel the prawns and cube the paneer. Blend the tomato purée, yogurt, garam masala, chilli powder, crushed garlic, salt, mango powder and ground coriander in a mixing bowl and set aside.

COOK'S TIP: Paneer is a useful ingredient in Indian dishes. It is available from most supermarkets.

2 Melt the butter or ghee with the corn oil in a wok or heavy-based frying pan. Lower the heat slightly and quickly fry the paneer cubes and prawns for about 2 minutes. Remove with a slotted spoon and drain thoroughly on kitchen paper.

3 Pour the spice mixture into the fat left in the pan and stir-fry for about 1 minute. Add the paneer and prawns and cook for 7–10 minutes, stirring occasionally, until the prawns are heated through.

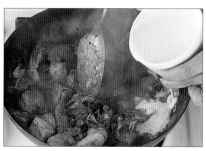

4 Add the chillies and most of the chopped fresh coriander and pour in the cream. Heat through for about 2 minutes, garnish with the remaining coriander and serve immediately.

King Prawns with Onion & Curry Leaves

Pungent fenugreek leaves give a final extra burst of flavour to this curry, which could hardly be quicker to make.

Serves 4

INGREDIENTS

3 medium onions
15 ml/1 tbsp corn oil
6–8 curry leaves
1.5 ml/¼ tsp onion seeds
1 green chilli, seeded and diced
1 red chilli, seeded and diced
12–14 frozen cooked king prawns (jumbo
    shrimp), thawed and peeled
5 ml/1 tsp grated fresh
    root ginger
5 ml/1 tsp salt
15 ml/1 tbsp fresh fenugreek leaves,
    plus extra to garnish
naan bread, to serve

2 Add the diced green and red chillies, followed by the prawns. Cook for about 5–7 minutes, then add the ginger and salt.

3 Finally add the fenugreek leaves. Cover the pan and cook for a further 2–3 minutes. Garnish with a few fenugreek leaves and serve with fresh, warm naan bread.

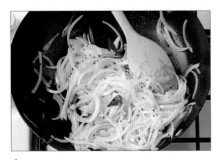

1 Slice the onions. Heat the oil in a non-stick wok or heavy-based frying pan and stir-fry the onions with the curry leaves and onion seeds for about 3 minutes.

VARIATION: If you like very hot curries you could include a few of the fiery chilli seeds in the dish.

Green Curry of Prawns

A fragrant, creamy Thai curry that takes very little time to prepare.

Serves 4–6

INGREDIENTS
30 ml/2 tbsp vegetable oil
30 ml/2 tbsp ready-made Thai green
   curry paste
450 g/1 lb raw king prawns (jumbo shrimp),
   peeled and deveined
4 kaffir lime leaves, torn
1 lemon grass stalk, bruised and chopped
250 ml/8 fl oz/1 cup coconut milk
30 ml/2 tbsp fish sauce
½ cucumber, seeded and cut into
   thin batons
10–15 fresh basil leaves
4 green chillies, sliced, to garnish

1 Heat the oil in a heavy-based frying pan. Add the green curry paste and fry until bubbling and fragrant.

COOK'S TIP: Thai green curry paste is a fragrant mixture of spices flavoured with lemon grass. It is available from supermarkets and can be used in a variety of dishes.

2 Add the prawns, kaffir lime leaves and lemon grass. Fry for 1–2 minutes until the prawns are pink.

3 Stir in the coconut milk and bring to a gentle boil. Simmer, stirring occasionally, for about 5 minutes or until the prawns are tender.

4 Stir in the fish sauce, cucumber and basil, then top with the sliced green chillies and serve.

VARIATION: Thin strips of chicken could also be used for this recipe.

Mussels & Clams with Lemon Grass & Coconut

The incomparable flavour of lemon grass is widely used in Thai cookery, especially seafood dishes such as this one.

Serves 6

INGREDIENTS
1.75 kg/4–4½ lb mussels
450 g/1 lb baby clams
120 ml/4 fl oz/½ cup dry
    white wine
1 bunch spring onions (scallions), chopped
2 lemon grass stalks, chopped
6 kaffir lime leaves, chopped
10 ml/2 tsp ready-made Thai
    green curry paste
200 ml/7 fl oz/scant 1 cup
    coconut cream
30 ml/2 tbsp chopped fresh coriander
    (cilantro)
salt and freshly ground black pepper
fresh garlic or ordinary chives,
    to garnish

1 Clean the mussels by scraping off the beards with a sharp knife, scrubbing their shells well and removing any barnacles. Discard any mussels that are broken or which do not close when tapped sharply. Rinse the mussels under several changes of water to remove any grit. Wash the clams.

> COOK'S TIP: Buy a few extra mussels in case there are any that have to be discarded.

2 Put the wine in a large saucepan with the spring onions, lemon grass, kaffir lime leaves and green curry paste. Simmer until the wine has almost evaporated.

3 Add the mussels and clams to the pan, cover tightly and steam over a high heat for 5–6 minutes until the shellfish are open.

4 Using a slotted spoon, transfer the cooked mussels and clams to a heated serving bowl and keep hot. Discard any shellfish that remain closed. Strain the cooking liquid into a clean pan and simmer to reduce to about 250 ml/8 fl oz/1 cup.

5 Stir in the coconut cream and coriander, with salt and pepper to taste. Heat through. Pour the sauce over the mussels and clams and serve, garnished with chives.

Kashmiri Chicken Curry

This north Indian dish is mild yet flavoursome and the addition of sliced apples give its creamy sauce a special lift.

Serves 4

INGREDIENTS
10 ml/2 tsp corn oil
2 medium onions, diced
1 bay leaf
2 cloves
2.5 cm/1 in cinnamon stick
4 black peppercorns
1 baby chicken, about 675 g/1½ lb,
   skinned and cut into 8 pieces
5 ml/1 tsp garam masala
5 ml/1 tsp grated fresh
   root ginger
5 ml/1 tsp crushed garlic
5 ml/1 tsp salt
5 ml/1 tsp chilli powder
15 ml/1 tbsp ground almonds
150 ml/¼ pint/⅔ cup natural (plain) yogurt
2 green eating apples, peeled, cored and
   roughly sliced
15 ml/1 tbsp chopped
   fresh coriander (cilantro)
15 g/½ oz/2 tbsp flaked almonds,
   lightly toasted, and fresh coriander
   (cilantro) leaves, to garnish

1 Heat the oil in a non-stick wok or heavy-based frying pan and fry the diced onions with the bay leaf, cloves, cinnamon and peppercorns for about 3–5 minutes. Add the chicken pieces and continue to stir-fry for at least 3 minutes.

2 Lower the heat and add the garam masala, ginger, garlic, salt, chilli powder and ground almonds and continue to stir-fry for 2–3 minutes.

3 Pour in the yogurt and cook, stirring, for a couple more minutes. Add the sliced apples and chopped coriander. Cover and cook over a gentle heat for about 10–15 minutes.

4 Check that the chicken is cooked through and serve immediately, garnished with the flaked almonds and whole coriander leaves.

Chicken in a Creamy Coconut Sauce

If you like the flavour of coconut, you will really love this curry.

Serves 4

INGREDIENTS

15 ml/1 tbsp ground almonds
15 ml/1 tbsp desiccated (dry unsweetened shredded) coconut
85 ml/3 fl oz/⅓ cup coconut milk
175 g/6 oz/⅔ cup fromage frais
7.5 ml/1½ tsp ground coriander
5 ml/1 tsp chilli powder
5 ml/1 tsp crushed garlic
7.5 ml/1½ tsp grated fresh root ginger
5 ml/1 tsp salt
15 ml/1 tbsp corn oil
375 g/13 oz skinned chicken, cubed
3 green cardamom pods
1 dried red chilli, crushed
30 ml/2 tbsp chopped fresh coriander (cilantro)

2 Add the coconut milk, fromage frais, ground coriander, chilli powder, crushed garlic, ginger and the salt to the almonds and coconut in the mixing bowl. Stir the mixture well.

3 Heat the oil in a non-stick wok or heavy-based frying pan and add the chicken cubes, and cardamoms. Stir-fry for approximately 2 minutes to seal the chicken.

4 Pour in the coconut milk mixture and blend everything together. Lower the heat, add the crushed chilli and fresh coriander, cover and cook for 10–12 minutes, stirring occasionally. Uncover, then stir and cook for a further 2 minutes before serving.

1 Using a heavy-based saucepan, dry fry the ground almonds and desiccated coconut until they turn a shade darker. Transfer the mixture to a mixing bowl.

COOK'S TIP: Cut the chicken into small, equal-size cubes for quick and even cooking.

Balti Chicken Curry

Tender pieces of chicken are lightly cooked with fresh vegetables and aromatic spices in the traditional balti style.

Serves 4

INGREDIENTS
675 g/1½ lb chicken breasts
30 ml/2 tbsp corn oil
2.5 ml/½ tsp cumin seeds
2.5 ml/½ tsp fennel seeds
1 onion, thickly sliced
2 garlic cloves, crushed
2.5 cm/1 in fresh root ginger,
   finely chopped
15 ml/1 tbsp curry paste
225 g/8 oz broccoli, broken
   into florets
4 tomatoes, cut into thick wedges
5 ml/1 tsp garam masala
30 ml/2 tbsp chopped fresh coriander
   (cilantro)
naan bread, to serve

2 Heat the oil in a wok and fry the cumin and fennel seeds for 2 minutes until the seeds begin to splutter. Add the onion, crushed garlic and chopped ginger and cook for 5–7 minutes. Stir in the curry paste and cook for a further 2–3 minutes.

3 Add the broccoli and fry for about 5 minutes. Add the chicken and fry for 5–8 minutes, stirring occasionally.

1 Remove the skin and any fat from the chicken and cut the meat into 2.5 cm/1 in cubes. Set aside.

4 Add the tomatoes, garam masala and chopped coriander. Cook for a further 5–10 minutes or until the chicken is tender. Serve with the naan bread.

Chilli Chicken

Hot and spicy would be the best way of describing this mouthwatering balti dish. Large green chillies are lightly cooked and smell delicious.

Serves 4–6

INGREDIENTS
75 ml/5 tbsp corn oil
8 large green chillies, slit
2.5 ml/½ tsp mixed onion and cumin seeds
4 curry leaves
5 ml/1 tsp grated fresh root ginger
5 ml/1 tsp chilli powder
5 ml/1 tsp ground coriander
5 ml/1 tsp crushed garlic
5 ml/1 tsp salt
2 medium onions, chopped
675 g/1½ lb chicken, skinned, boned and cubed
15 ml/1 tbsp lemon juice
15 ml/1 tbsp roughly chopped fresh mint
15 ml/1 tbsp roughly chopped fresh coriander (cilantro)
8–10 cherry tomatoes
naan bread or paratha, to serve

2 Add the onion and cumin seeds, curry leaves, ginger, chilli powder, ground coriander, garlic, salt and onions and fry for a few seconds, stirring continuously.

3 Add the cubed chicken and stir-fry for 10 minutes or until the chicken is cooked right through.

4 Sprinkle on the lemon juice and add the mint and coriander. Return the green chillies to the pan and heat through, stirring gently. Add the cherry tomatoes and serve with naan bread or paratha.

1 Heat the oil in a wok or heavy-based frying pan and add the chillies. Fry until the skin changes colour then remove.

Chicken with Cashew Nuts

This chicken dish has a deliciously thick and nutty sauce, and it is best served with plain boiled rice.

Serves 4

INGREDIENTS

2 medium onions
30 ml/2 tbsp tomato purée (paste)
50 g/2 oz/⅓ cup cashew nuts
7.5 ml/1½ tsp garam masala
5 ml/1 tsp crushed garlic
5 ml/1 tsp chilli powder
1.5 ml/¼ tsp ground turmeric
5 ml/1 tsp salt
15 ml/1 tbsp lemon juice
15 ml/1 tbsp natural (plain) yogurt
30 ml/2 tbsp corn oil
30 ml/2 tbsp chopped fresh coriander
   (cilantro)
15 ml/1 tbsp sultanas (golden raisins)
450 g/1 lb chicken, skinned, boned and cubed
175 g/6 oz/2½ cups button (white)
   mushrooms
300 ml/½ pint/1¼ cups water

1 Process the onions for 1 minute. Add the tomato purée, nuts, spices, salt, lemon juice and yogurt and process for a further 1–1½ minutes.

2 Heat the oil in a saucepan. Lower the heat to medium and pour in the spice mixture from the food processor or blender. Fry for about 2 minutes, lowering the heat if necessary and stirring frequently.

3 Add 15 ml/1 tbsp of the fresh chopped coriander, the sultanas and the cubed chicken to the saucepan. Continue to stir-fry for a further 1 minute, ensuring that the chicken is well coated with the spice mixture.

4 Add the mushrooms, pour in the water and bring to a simmer. Cover the saucepan and cook over a low heat for about 10 minutes.

5 Check that the chicken is cooked through and tender and the sauce is thick. Cook for a little longer if necessary. Serve garnished with the remaining coriander.

Chicken with Paneer & Peas

The unusual combination of chicken and paneer works well in this dish with its deliciously spicy sauce. Serve with plain boiled rice.

Serves 4

INGREDIENTS

1 baby chicken, about 675 g/1½ lb
30 ml/2 tbsp tomato purée (paste)
45 ml/3 tbsp natural (plain) yogurt
7.5 ml/1½ tsp garam masala
5 ml/1 tsp crushed garlic
5 ml/1 tsp grated fresh
   root ginger
pinch of ground cardamom
15 ml/1 tbsp chilli powder
1.5 ml/¼ tsp ground turmeric
5 ml/1 tsp salt
5 ml/1 tsp sugar
10 ml/2 tsp corn oil
2.5 cm/1 in cinnamon stick
2 black peppercorns
300 ml/½ pint/1¼ cups water
115 g/4 oz paneer cheese, cubed
30 ml/2 tbsp fresh coriander (cilantro) leaves
2 green chillies, seeded
   and chopped
50 g/2 oz/¼ cup fromage frais
75 g/3 oz/¾ cup frozen
   peas, thawed

1 Skin the chicken and cut it into six to eight pieces. Set aside until required. Place the tomato purée, yogurt, garam masala, crushed garlic, ginger, ground cardamom, chilli powder, turmeric, salt and sugar in a bowl and mix together well.

2 Heat the oil with the whole spices in a non-stick wok or heavy-based frying pan, then pour the sauce mixture into the oil. Lower the heat and cook for about 3 minutes, then pour in the water.

3 Add the chicken pieces and cook, stirring, for about 2 minutes, then cover and cook over a medium heat for about 10 minutes.

4 Add the paneer cubes to the pan, followed by half the coriander leaves and half the green chillies. Stir to mix everything well and cook for a further 5-7 minutes.

5 Stir in the fromage frais and peas, heat through, then serve, garnished with the remaining coriander and chopped chillies.

Chicken Madras

This is a fairly hot chicken curry which is good served with either plain boiled rice, pilau rice or naan bread.

Serves 4

INGREDIENTS
275 g/10 oz boned, skinless
  chicken breasts
45 ml/3 tbsp tomato purée (paste)
large pinch of ground fenugreek
1.5 ml/¼ tsp ground fennel seeds
5 ml/1 tsp grated fresh
  root ginger
7.5 ml/1½ tsp ground coriander
5 ml/1 tsp crushed garlic
5 ml/1 tsp chilli powder
1.5 ml/¼ tsp ground turmeric
30 ml/2 tbsp lemon juice
5 ml/1 tsp salt
300 ml/½ pint/1¼ cups water
15 ml/1 tbsp corn oil
2 medium onions, diced
2–4 curry leaves
2 green chillies, seeded and chopped
15 ml/1 tbsp fresh coriander (cilantro) leaves

1 Cut the chicken breasts into bite-size cubes. Set aside until required. Place the tomato purée in a bowl with the fenugreek, fennel seeds, ginger, ground coriander, garlic, chilli powder, turmeric, lemon juice, salt and water.

COOK'S TIP: Always take care not to be over-generous when you are using ground fenugreek, as it can be quite bitter.

2 Heat the oil in a non-stick wok or heavy-based frying pan and stir-fry the onions until they are golden brown. Add the curry leaves and stir-fry briefly.

3 Add the cubed chicken to the onions and stir-fry for about 1 minute to seal the meat. Pour the sauce into the wok or pan and continue to cook, stirring, for about 2 minutes to coat the chicken.

4 Lower the heat and cook the curry for 8–10 minutes, stirring occasionally. Add the chopped chillies and fresh coriander and serve.

Balti Chicken in a Spicy Lentil Sauce

Tarka, a seasoned oil, is poured over this dish just before serving, giving it an extra spicy boost. Serve with boiled rice or naan bread.

Serves 4

INGREDIENTS
30 ml/2 tbsp chana dhal
50 g/2 oz/¼ cup masoor dhal
15 ml/1 tbsp corn oil
2 medium onions, chopped
5 ml/1 tsp crushed garlic
5 ml/1 tsp grated fresh root ginger
2.5 ml/½ tsp ground turmeric
7.5 ml/1½ tsp chilli powder
5 ml/1 tsp garam masala
2.5 ml/½ tsp ground coriander
7.5 ml/1½ tsp salt
175 g/6 oz skinless chicken breasts,
    boned and cubed
45 ml/3 tbsp fresh coriander (cilantro) leaves
1–2 green chillies, seeded
    and chopped
30–45 ml/2–3 tbsp lemon juice
300 ml/½ pint/1¼ cups water
2 tomatoes, skinned and halved

FOR THE TARKA
5 ml/1 tsp corn oil
2.5 ml/½ tsp cumin seeds
2 garlic cloves
2 dried red chillies
4 curry leaves

1 Boil the chana dhal and masoor dhal together in a saucepan of water until soft and mushy. Set aside.

2 Heat the oil in a non-stick wok or heavy-based frying pan and fry the onions until soft and golden brown. Stir in the garlic, ginger, turmeric, chilli powder, garam masala, ground coriander and salt.

3 Next, add the cubed chicken and stir-fry for 5–7 minutes. Add half the fresh coriander, the green chillies, lemon juice and water and cook for a further 3–5 minutes. Stir in the dhal, followed by the tomatoes. Add the remaining fresh coriander. Remove from the heat and set aside.

4 To make the tarka, heat the oil and add the cumin seeds, whole garlic cloves, dried chillies and curry leaves. Heat for about 30 seconds and, while it is still hot, pour it over the top of the dhal. Serve immediately.

VARIATION: If you want to make this a vegetarian dish, just replace the chicken with the same quantity of vegetables of your choice.

Creamy Lamb Korma

Cutting the lamb into strips for this lovely dish makes it easier to cook.

Serves 4

INGREDIENTS
3 green chillies
120 ml/4 fl oz/½ cup natural (plain) yogurt
50 ml/2 fl oz/¼ cup coconut milk
15 ml/1 tbsp ground almonds
5 ml/1 tsp salt
5 ml/1 tsp crushed garlic
5 ml/1 tsp grated fresh root ginger
5 ml/1 tsp garam masala
1.5 ml/¼ tsp ground cardamom
large pinch of ground cinnamon
15 ml/1 tbsp chopped fresh mint
15 ml/1 tbsp corn oil
2 medium onions, diced
1 bay leaf
4 black peppercorns
225 g/8 oz lean lamb, cut into strips
150 ml/¼ pint/⅔ cup water
fresh mint leaves, to garnish

1 Seed and finely chop two chillies. Whisk into the yogurt with the coconut milk, ground almonds, salt, garlic, ginger, garam masala, cardamom, cinnamon and chopped mint.

2 Seed the remaining green chilli and slice into strips. Set aside.

3 Heat the oil in a non-stick wok or heavy-based frying pan and stir-fry the diced onions with the bay leaf and peppercorns.

4 When the onions are soft and golden brown, add the strips of lamb and stir-fry for about 2 minutes.

5 Pour in the yogurt mixture and water, lower the heat, cover and cook for about 15 minutes or until the lamb is cooked through, stirring occasionally. Stir-fry for a further 2 minutes. Serve garnished with chilli strips and mint.

Balti Keema with Curry Leaves & Green Chillies

Minced lamb is cooked in its own juices with a few spices and herbs, but no other liquid. Naan bread makes an ideal accompaniment.

Serves 4

INGREDIENTS
10 ml/2 tsp corn oil
2 medium onions, chopped
10 curry leaves
6 green chillies
350 g/12 oz lean minced (ground) lamb
5 ml/1 tsp crushed garlic
5 ml/1 tsp grated fresh root ginger
5 ml/1 tsp chilli powder
1.5 ml/¼ tsp ground turmeric
5 ml/1 tsp salt
2 tomatoes, peeled and quartered
15 ml/1 tbsp chopped fresh coriander
　(cilantro)

2 Put the minced lamb into a bowl and add the garlic, ginger, chilli powder, turmeric and salt. Blend everything thoroughly.

3 Tip the lamb mixture into the fried onion mixture and stir-fry for 7–10 minutes, lowering the heat to medium if necessary.

1 Heat the oil in a non-stick wok or heavy-based frying pan and fry the onions together with the curry leaves and three whole green chillies.

4 Add the quartered tomatoes and chopped coriander and the remaining whole green chillies. Continue to stir-fry for a further 2 minutes before serving.

Lamb Curry with Cauliflower

Cauliflower and lamb go beautifully together. This dish is given a final topping of cumin seeds and curry leaves, which enhances the flavour.

Serves 4

INGREDIENTS
10 ml/2 tsp corn oil
2 medium onions, sliced
7.5 ml/1½ tsp grated fresh root ginger
5 ml/1 tsp chilli powder
5 ml/1 tsp crushed garlic
1.5 ml/¼ tsp ground turmeric
2.5 ml/½ tsp ground coriander
30 ml/2 tbsp fresh fenugreek leaves
275 g/10 oz boned lean spring lamb,
    cut into strips
1 small cauliflower, cut into small florets
300 ml/½ pint/1¼ cups water
30 ml/2 tbsp fresh coriander (cilantro) leaves
½ red pepper, seeded and sliced
15 ml/1 tbsp lemon juice

FOR THE TARKA
10 ml/2 tsp corn oil
2.5 ml/½ tsp white cumin seeds
4–6 curry leaves

1 Heat the oil in a non-stick wok or heavy-based frying pan and fry the onions until golden brown. Lower the heat and add the ginger, chilli powder, garlic, turmeric and ground coriander, followed by the fenugreek.

COOK'S TIP: A tarka is a blend of lightly fried spices added at the end of cooking.

2 Add the lamb strips to the wok and stir-fry until the lamb is completely coated with the spices. Add half the cauliflower florets and stir the mixture well to combine.

3 Pour in the water, cover the wok tightly, lower the heat and cook for 5–7 minutes until the cauliflower and lamb are almost cooked through.

4 Add the remaining cauliflower, half the fresh coriander, the sliced red pepper and lemon juice and cook, stirring, for about 5 minutes, ensuring that the sauce does not catch on the bottom of the wok.

5 Check that the lamb is completely cooked by piercing with a sharp knife, and cook for a little longer if necessary. Remove the wok from the heat and set aside to keep warm while you make the tarka.

6 To make the tarka, heat the oil and fry the cumin seeds and curry leaves for about 30 seconds. While it is still hot, pour the seasoned oil over the cauliflower and lamb and serve garnished with the remaining fresh coriander leaves.

Lamb Masala Keema

A rather spicy, dry keema, which combines the warm flavours of
cardamom, cinnamon and cloves. Serve with rice or chapattis.

Serves 4

INGREDIENTS

15 ml/1 tbsp corn oil
2 cardamom pods
2.5 cm/1 in cinnamon stick
2 cloves
3 black peppercorns
3 medium onions, chopped
350 g/12 oz lean minced (ground) lamb
7.5 ml/1½ tsp garam masala
5 ml/1 tsp chilli powder
5 ml/1 tsp crushed garlic
7.5 ml/1½ tsp grated fresh
    root ginger
5 ml/1 tsp salt
1 large potato, cut into small cubes
2 tomatoes, peeled and diced
30 ml/2 tbsp fresh coriander (cilantro) leaves

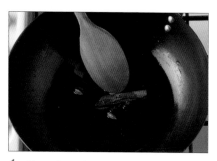

1 Heat the oil in a non-stick wok or
heavy-based frying pan and fry the
whole spices for about 1 minute. Add
the onions and continue to fry for a
further 3 minutes.

2 Meanwhile put the lamb into a
bowl and mix in the garam masala,
chilli powder, garlic, ginger and salt.

3 Tip the lamb mixture into the
onions and spices and stir-fry for
5–7 minutes, taking care to break up
any lumps of meat that stick together
and mixing to combine.

4 Add the potato and tomatoes.
Chop half the coriander leaves and
add these. Cover the wok or pan and
cook over a low heat for 3–5 minutes
so that the potato is cooked in the
steam. Garnish with the remaining
coriander leaves and serve.

Citrus Beef Curry

This superbly aromatic Thai-style curry is not too hot, but is full of flavour. For a special meal, it goes perfectly with Thai fried noodles.

Serves 4

INGREDIENTS
30 ml/2 tbsp oil
30 ml/2 tbsp medium curry paste
450 g/1 lb lean rump steak, cut into
    5 cm/2 in strips
2 bay leaves
400 ml/14 fl oz/1⅔ cups coconut milk
300 ml/½ pint/1¼ cups beef stock
30 ml/2 tbsp lemon juice
45 ml/3 tbsp Thai fish sauce
15 ml/1 tbsp caster (superfine) sugar
115 g/4 oz baby (pearl) onions, peeled
    but left whole
225 g/8 oz new potatoes, halved
115 g/4 oz/1 cup unsalted roasted peanuts,
    roughly chopped
115 g/4 oz fine green beans, halved
1 red (bell) pepper, seeded and
    thinly sliced
unsalted roasted peanuts,
    to garnish (optional)

1 Heat the oil in a heavy-based saucepan and cook the curry paste over a medium heat for 30 seconds.

2 Stir in the beef and cook it for 2 minutes until it is beginning to brown and is coated with the spices.

3 Stir in the bay leaves, coconut milk, stock, lemon juice, fish sauce and sugar. Bring to the boil, stirring.

4 Add the baby onions and halved potatoes, then bring back to the boil, reduce the heat and leave to simmer, uncovered, for 5 minutes.

5 Stir in the peanuts, green beans and red pepper and simmer for a further 10 minutes or until the beef and potatoes are tender. Cook for a little longer, if necessary.

6 Serve the curry in shallow bowls, with a spoon and fork, to enjoy all the rich and creamy juices. Sprinkle with extra unsalted roasted peanuts, if you wish.

Beef & Coconut Curry

This simple dish makes good use of traditional Indian spices to produce a creamy, flavoursome curry with a hint of coconut.

Serves 4

INGREDIENTS

15 ml/1 tbsp oil
450 g/1 lb minced (ground) beef
2 garlic cloves, chopped
5 ml/1 tsp ground cumin
5 ml/1 tsp ground coriander
5 ml/1 tsp garam masala
1 cm/½ in fresh root ginger,
   peeled and chopped
40 g/1½ oz/3 tbsp ground almonds
175 ml/6 fl oz/¾ cup coconut milk
120 ml/4 fl oz/½ cup beef stock
30 ml/2 tbsp chopped fresh coriander
   (cilantro)
225 g/8 oz/generous 1 cup long grain rice
5 ml/1 tsp ground turmeric
15 g/½ oz/2 tbsp flaked almonds
salt and ground black pepper
fresh coriander (cilantro) and cream, to
   garnish

3 Reduce the heat and simmer gently for 20 minutes. Stir in the chopped fresh coriander.

1 Heat the oil in a heavy-based frying pan and fry the minced beef and garlic for 5 minutes. Add the cumin, ground coriander, garam masala and ginger. Cook for a further 2 minutes.

2 Add 25 g/1 oz/2 tbsp ground almonds, season well and stir. Pour in the coconut milk and beef stock. Mix well and bring to the boil.

4 Meanwhile, cook the rice in boiling salted water for 10–12 minutes or until *al dente*. Drain well. Return to the pan and stir in the turmeric and flaked almonds. Serve with the coconut curry, garnished with a sprig of fresh coriander and cream sprinkled with ground almonds.

Balti Beef

If you don't have a *karahi*, you can use a wok or large heavy-based frying pan to cook this aromatic dish.

Serves 4

INGREDIENTS
1 red (bell) pepper
1 green (bell) pepper
30 ml/2 tbsp oil
5 ml/1 tsp cumin seeds
2.5 ml/½ tsp fennel seeds
1 onion, cut into thick wedges
1 garlic clove, crushed
2.5 cm/1 in piece fresh
   root ginger, peeled and
   finely chopped
1 red chilli, finely chopped
15 ml/1 tbsp curry paste
2.5 ml/½ tsp salt
675 g/1½ lb rump or fillet steak,
   cut into thick strips
coriander naan bread, to serve

2 Heat the oil in a wok or heavy-based frying pan and fry the cumin and fennel seeds for about 2 minutes or until they begin to splutter. Add the onion, garlic, ginger and chilli and fry for 5 minutes.

3 Add the curry paste and salt and fry for a further 3–4 minutes. Add the red and green peppers and stir-fry for about 5 minutes.

1 Halve the red and green peppers and discard the seeds and core. Cut into 2.5 cm/1 in chunks and set them aside.

4 Stir in the beef and continue to fry for 10–12 minutes or until the meat is tender. Serve with warm coriander naan bread.

Aloo Saag

Spinach, potatoes and traditional Indian spices are the main ingredients in this simple, delicious and authentic curry.

Serves 4

INGREDIENTS
450 g/1 lb spinach
30 ml/2 tbsp oil
5 ml/1 tsp black mustard seeds
1 onion, thinly sliced
2 garlic cloves, crushed
2.5 cm/1 in fresh root ginger,
    peeled and finely chopped
675 g/1½ lb potatoes, cut into
    2.5 cm/1 in chunks
5 ml/1 tsp chilli powder
5 ml/1 tsp salt
120 ml/4 fl oz/½ cup water

3 Heat the oil in a large saucepan and fry the mustard seeds for 2 minutes or until they begin to splutter.

1 Wash the spinach in several changes of cold water, then blanch in boiling water for 3–4 minutes.

2 Drain the spinach thoroughly and set aside. When it is cool enough to handle, use your hands to squeeze out any remaining liquid.

4 Add the onion, garlic and ginger and fry for 5 minutes, stirring. Add the potatoes, chilli powder, salt and water and cook for 8 minutes.

COOK'S TIPS: To make certain that the spinach is dry, put it in a clean dish towel, roll up tightly and squeeze gently to remove any excess liquid.
    Use a waxy variety of potato for this dish so that the pieces do not break up during cooking.

5 Add the drained spinach. Cover the saucepan with a tight-fitting lid and simmer for 10–15 minutes or until the potatoes are tender. Serve hot.

Cauliflower with Tomatoes

Serves 4

INGREDIENTS
30 ml/2 tbsp vegetable oil
1 onion, chopped
2 garlic cloves, crushed
1 cauliflower, broken into florets
5 ml/1 tsp ground coriander
5 ml/1 tsp ground cumin
5 ml/1 tsp ground fennel seeds
2.5 ml/½ tsp garam masala
pinch of ground ginger
2.5 ml/½ tsp chilli powder
4 plum tomatoes, peeled,
    seeded and quartered
175 ml/6 fl oz/¾ cup water
175 g/6 oz spinach, roughly chopped
15–30 ml/1–2 tbsp lemon juice
salt and ground black pepper

1 Heat the oil in a wok or heavy-based frying pan. Add the onion and garlic and stir-fry for 2–3 minutes over a high heat until the onion begins to brown. Add the cauliflower florets and stir-fry for a further 2–3 minutes until the cauliflower is flecked with brown.

2 Add the coriander, cumin, fennel seeds, garam masala, ginger and chilli powder and cook over a high heat for 1 minute, stirring all the time. Add the tomatoes, water and salt and pepper. Bring to the boil, then reduce the heat, cover and simmer for 5–6 minutes until the cauliflower is just tender.

3 Stir in the spinach, cover and cook for 1 minute. Add enough lemon juice to sharpen the flavour. Serve.

Masala Okra

This popular Indian vegetable is stir-fried with a dry, spicy masala to make a delicious side dish.

Serves 4

INGREDIENTS

450 g/1 lb okra
2.5 ml/½ tsp ground turmeric
5 ml/1 tsp chilli powder
15 ml/1 tbsp ground cumin
15 ml/1 tbsp ground coriander
1.5 ml/¼ tsp sugar
15 ml/1 tbsp lemon juice
15 ml/1 tbsp desiccated (dry unsweetened
   shredded) coconut
30 ml/2 tbsp chopped fresh coriander
   (cilantro)
45 ml/3 tbsp oil
2.5 ml/½ tsp cumin seeds
2.5 ml/½ tsp black mustard seeds
chopped fresh tomatoes, to garnish
poppadums, to serve

1 Wash, dry and trim the okra. In a bowl, mix together the turmeric, chilli powder, cumin, ground coriander, sugar, lemon juice, desiccated coconut and fresh coriander.

2 Heat the oil in a heavy-based frying pan. Add the cumin seeds and mustard seeds and fry for about 2 minutes or until they begin to splutter. Add the spice mixture and continue to fry for 2 minutes more.

3 Add the okra, cover and cook over a low heat for 10 minutes or until tender. Garnish with plenty of chopped fresh tomatoes and serve with warmed poppadums.

Vegetable Kashmiri

In this tasty curry, fresh mixed vegetables are cooked in a spicy, aromatic yogurt sauce. Use small okra for the tenderest texture.

Serves 4

INGREDIENTS
10 ml/2 tsp cumin seeds
8 black peppercorns
2 green cardamom pods, seeds only
5 cm/2 in cinnamon stick
2.5 ml/½ tsp grated nutmeg
45 ml/3 tbsp oil
1 green chilli, chopped
2.5 cm/1 in fresh root ginger,
   peeled and grated
5 ml/1 tsp chilli powder
2.5 ml/½ tsp salt
2 large potatoes, cut into
   2.5 cm/1 in chunks
225 g/8 oz cauliflower, broken
   into florets
225 g/8 oz okra, thickly sliced
150 ml/¼ pint/⅔ cup natural (plain) yogurt
150 ml/¼ pint/⅔ cup
   vegetable stock
toasted flaked almonds and fresh
   coriander (cilantro) sprigs, to garnish

1 Grind the cumin seeds, peppercorns, cardamom seeds, cinnamon stick and nutmeg to a fine powder using a food processor or a pestle and mortar.

2 Heat the oil in a large, heavy-based saucepan and fry the green chilli and grated ginger for 2 minutes, stirring all the time.

3 Add the chilli powder, salt and ground spice mixture and fry for about 2–3 minutes, stirring constantly to prevent the spices from sticking.

4 Stir in the potatoes, cover and cook for 10 minutes over a low heat, stirring from time to time. Add the cauliflower and okra and cook for 5 minutes, stirring to mix with the spices.

5 Add the yogurt and stock. Bring to the boil, then reduce the heat. Cover and simmer for 20 minutes or until all the vegetables are tender. Garnish with toasted almonds and coriander sprigs before serving.

Thai Tofu Curry

A marvellous mixture of Chinese and Indian influences plus other exotic ingredients are combined in this Thai dish.

Serves 4

INGREDIENTS
2 x 200 g/7 oz packs tofu, cubed
30 ml/2 tbsp light soy sauce
30 ml/2 tbsp groundnut oil
thin slices of red chilli or
    red pepper and lime slices,
    to garnish
Thai fragrant or jasmine rice,
    to serve

FOR THE PASTE
1 small onion, chopped
2 green chillies, seeded and chopped
2 garlic cloves, chopped
15 ml/1 tbsp grated fresh galangal
    or 5 ml/1 tsp grated fresh
    root ginger
2 kaffir lime leaves or 5 ml/1 tsp
    grated lime rind
10 ml/2 tsp coriander seeds, crushed
10 ml/2 tsp cumin seeds, crushed
45 ml/3 tbsp chopped fresh coriander
    (cilantro)
15 ml/1 tbsp Thai fish sauce or
    soy sauce
juice of 1 lime or small lemon
5 ml/1 tsp sugar
25 g/1 oz creamed coconut dissolved in
    150 ml/¼ pint/⅔ cup boiling water, or
    30 ml/2 tbsp coconut cream

1 Toss the tofu cubes in soy sauce and leave to marinate for about 15 minutes. Meanwhile, put all the paste ingredients into a food processor and process until smooth.

2 Heat the oil in a wok or heavy-based frying pan until quite hot. Drain the tofu cubes and stir-fry at a high temperature until well browned on all sides and just firm. Remove and drain on kitchen paper and keep warm.

3 Wipe the wok clean with kitchen paper. Pour in the paste and stir well. Return the tofu to the wok and mix it into the paste to reheat.

4 Transfer to a flat serving platter and garnish with sliced red chilli or pepper and lime slices. Serve with Thai fragrant or jasmine rice.

COOK'S TIP: The paste and marinated tofu could be prepared in advance, if preferred.

Tarka Dhal

Dhal is cooked in every house in India in one form or another.

Serves 4–6

INGREDIENTS
115 g/4 oz/½ cup red lentils, washed
50 g/2 oz/¼ cup split yellow lentils, washed
350 ml/12 fl oz/1½ cups water
4 green chillies
5 ml/1 tsp ground turmeric
1 large onion, sliced
400 g/14 oz can plum tomatoes, crushed
salt

FOR THE TARKA
60 ml/4 tbsp vegetable oil
2.5 ml/½ tsp mustard and cumin seeds
1 garlic clove, sliced
6 curry leaves
2 dried red chillies
1.5 ml/¼ tsp asafoetida

1 Place the lentils, water, green chillies, turmeric and onion in a heavy-based pan and bring to the boil. Simmer, covered, for 30 minutes or until the lentils are soft and the water has evaporated.

2 Mash the lentils with the back of a spoon. When nearly smooth, mix in the tomatoes and salt to taste. Thin the mixture with hot water, if necessary.

3 To make the tarka, heat the oil in a heavy-based frying pan and fry the mustard and cumin seeds, garlic slices, curry leaves, chillies and asafoetida, until the garlic browns. Pour the mixture over the lentils, cover and let stand for 5 minutes. Stir well and serve.

Kidney Bean Curry

This is a very popular Punjabi-style dish using red kidney beans.

Serves 4

INGREDIENTS
30 ml/2 tbsp oil
2.5 ml/½ tsp cumin seeds
1 onion, thinly sliced
1 green chilli, finely chopped
2 garlic cloves, crushed
2.5 cm/1 in fresh root ginger, peeled
    and grated
30 ml/2 tbsp curry paste
5 ml/1 tsp ground cumin
5 ml/1 tsp ground coriander
2.5 ml/½ tsp chilli powder
400 g/14 oz can chopped tomatoes
3 x 225 g/8 oz cans red kidney beans,
    drained and rinsed
30 ml/2 tbsp chopped fresh coriander
    (cilantro)

1 Heat the oil in a large, heavy-based frying pan, add the cumin seeds and fry for 2 minutes or until they begin to splutter.

2 Add the onion, chilli, garlic and ginger and fry for 5 minutes. Stir in the curry paste, ground cumin and coriander, and chilli powder and cook for 5 minutes.

3 Add the chopped tomatoes and simmer for 5 minutes. Add the kidney beans and fresh coriander, reserving a little for the garnish. Cover and cook over gentle heat for 15 minutes, adding a little water if necessary. Serve immediately, garnished with the reserved coriander.

Indonesian Coconut Rice

This way of cooking rice is very popular throughout the whole of Southeast Asia. Coconut rice goes particularly well with fish, chicken and pork.

Serves 4–6

INGREDIENTS
350 g/12 oz/1¾ cups Thai fragrant rice
400 ml/14 fl oz can coconut milk
300 ml/½ pint/1¼ cups water
2.5 ml/½ tsp ground coriander
5 cm/2 in cinnamon stick
1 lemon grass stalk, bruised
1 bay leaf
salt
deep fried onions, to garnish

1 Put the rice in a strainer and rinse thoroughly under cold water. Drain well, then put in a pan. Pour in the coconut milk and water. Add the coriander, cinnamon stick, lemon grass and bay leaf. Season with salt. Bring to the boil, then lower the heat, cover and simmer for 8–10 minutes.

2 Lift the lid and check that all the liquid has been absorbed, then stir the rice through carefully with a fork, removing the cinnamon stick, lemon grass and bay leaf.

3 Cover the pan with a tight-fitting lid and continue to cook over the lowest possible heat for 3–5 minutes more.

4 Pile the rice on to a warm serving dish and serve garnished with the crisp, deep fried onions.

COOK'S TIP: When bringing the rice to the boil, stir it frequently. Once the rice is nearly tender, cover tightly and continue to cook over a very low heat or just leave to stand for 5 minutes.

Plain Rice

Vegetable oil added to rice enhances its natural flavour.

Serves 4–6

INGREDIENTS
400 g/14 oz/2 cups long grain rice
15 ml/1 tbsp vegetable oil
750 ml/1¼ pints/3 cups boiling water
2.5 ml/½ tsp salt

1 Wash and drain the rice several times in cold water until the water is no longer starchy. Put the rice in a heavy-based saucepan, add the vegetable oil, water and salt. Stir once to prevent the rice from sticking to the pan and simmer for 10–12 minutes.

2 Remove the saucepan from the heat, cover and allow the rice to steam in its own heat for a further 5 minutes. Fluff the rice with a fork or chopsticks before serving.

Index

This edition is published by Lorenz Books,
an imprint of Anness Publishing Ltd,
108 Great Russell Street, London WC1B 3NA info@anness.com

www.lorenzbooks.com; www.annesspublishing.com

© Anness Publishing Limited 2014

If you like the images in this book and would like to investigate using them for publishing, promotions or advertising, please visit our website www.practicalpictures.com for more information.

Publisher: Joanna Lorenz
Editor: Valerie Ferguson & Helen Sudell
Series Designer: Bobbie Colgate Stone
Designer: Andrew Heath

Recipes contributed by: Kit Chan,
Roz Denny, Nicola Diggins, Sarah Edmonds, Rafi Fernandez,
Shehzad Husain, Christine Ingram, Manisha Kanani, Lesley
Mackley, Sallie Morris, Jenny Stacey.

Photography: William Adams-Lingwood, David Armstrong,
Edward Allwright, David Jordan, Ferguson Hill, Michael
Michaels, Patrick McLeavy, Thomas Odulate

A CIP catalogue record for this book is available from the
British Library

COOK'S NOTES

Bracketed terms are intended for American readers.

For all recipes, quantities are given in both metric and imperial measures and, where appropriate, in standard cups and spoons. Follow one set of measures, but not a mixture, because they are not interchangeable.

Standard spoon and cup measures are level. 1 tsp = 5ml, 1 tbsp = 15ml, 1 cup = 250ml/8fl oz. Australian standard tablespoons are 20ml. Australian readers should use 3 tsp in place of 1 tbsp for measuring small quantities.

American pints are 16fl oz/2 cups. American readers should use 20fl oz/2.5 cups in place of 1 pint when measuring liquids.

Electric oven temperatures in this book are for conventional ovens. When using a fan oven, the temperature will probably need to be reduced by about 10–20°C/20–40°F. Since ovens vary, you should check with your manufacturer's instruction book for guidance.

Medium (US large) eggs are used unless otherwise stated.

PUBLISHER'S NOTE:

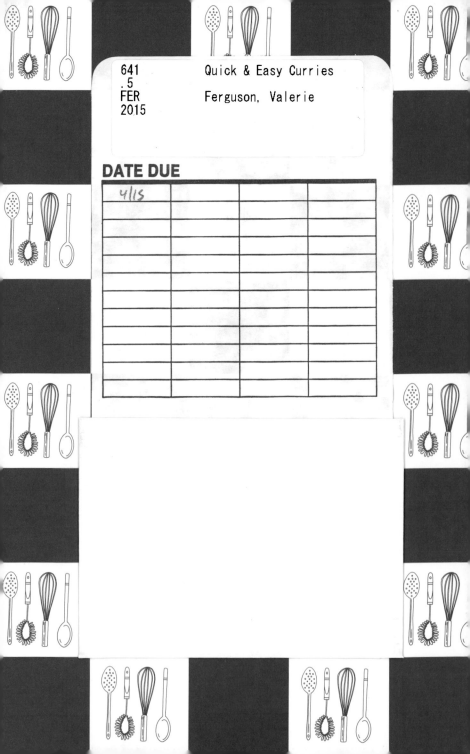

641
.5
FER
2015

Quick & Easy Curries

Ferguson, Valerie

DATE DUE

4/15			